Glycemic Index Cookbook

Glycemic Index Cookbook

Healthy cooking for your best health

Gina Steer, Sian Lewis, and Charlotte Watts

This edition published in 2010
LOVE FOOD is an imprint of Parragon Books Ltd

Parragon
Queen Street House
4 Queen Street
Bath BA1 1HE, UK

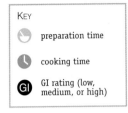

KEY

⊙ preparation time

🕐 cooking time

GI GI rating (low, medium, or high)

ISBN: 978-1-4454-2404-0

Printed in China

Produced by the Bridgewater Book Company Ltd

Recipe photography: Clive Bozzard-Hill
Home economist: Sue Henderson

Notes for the Reader
This book uses imperial, metric, and US cup measurements. Follow the
same units of measurement throughout; do not mix imperial and metric. All
spoon measurements are level: teaspoons are assumed to be 5 ml, and
tablespoons are assumed to be 15 ml. Unless otherwise stated, milk is
assumed to be whole, eggs and individual vegetables such as potatoes are
medium, and pepper is freshly ground black pepper.

The times given are an approximate guide only. Preparation times differ
according to the techniques used by different people and the cooking times
may also vary from those given as a result of the type of oven used. Optional
ingredients, variations or serving suggestions have not been included in the
calculations.

Recipes using raw or very lightly cooked eggs should be avoided by infants, the
elderly, pregnant women, convalescents, and anyone with a chronic condition.
Pregnant and breastfeeding women are advised to avoid eating peanuts and peanut
products. Sufferers from nut allergies should be aware that some of the ready-prepared
ingredients used in the recipes in this book may contain nuts. Always check the packaging
before use.

Vegetarians should be aware that some of the ready-prepared ingredients used in the recipes in
this book may contain animal products. Always check the packaging before use.

Picture acknowledgments
The Bridgewater Book Company would like to thank The Ivy Press Limited for permission to
reproduce copyright material on pages 11 (nuts), 12, 13, 15.

Contents

Introduction

The GI diet is an exciting new way of eating for a healthier lifestyle, offering a solution to the common problem of losing weight while still following a well-balanced diet.

We are all increasingly aware of good nutrition and its connection with health. With clinical obesity on the increase, both in adults and, more worryingly, in children, it is no surprise that diet-related cookbooks have become incredibly popular. While some of these books concentrate primarily on the problems of excess weight, this book goes farther by viewing the issue of losing weight within the wider context of an overall healthy lifestyle. Furthermore, unlike some diets, it avoids setting idealistic goals that can be difficult to follow, recommending a diet that is either expensive or unrealistic, or which cuts out some everyday foods. Finally, with so-called "magic" or "crash" diets, the weight quickly piles back on once these foods are re-introduced when the diet is over—the GI diet avoids the crash, and by changing the way you balance your foods for life, it may never really end as other diets do.

Nutrition is an issue for us all and the link between a healthy life and what we eat has long been recognized by both doctors and nutritionists alike. Eating correctly reduces the risk of heart disease, stroke, diabetes, obesity, and some food allergies, and can help in the fight against cancer. However, there are many conflicting messages in the media regarding the link between diet and good health, and it is easy to get confused. The fast-food culture is now an integral part of life, and it is all too easy to opt for a take-out, as time is short. This book helps to provide the answer, offering quick, simple recipes that are ideal when pursuing a healthy diet and lifestyle.

The first chapter of this book reveals the mysteries of the GI (Glycemic Index) table, highlighting foods that should be eaten on a daily basis in order to meet the energy demands we need, plus explaining why it is important not to cut out fat altogether from your diet but to choose sensible amounts of the right types—a quality, not quantity issue.

This chapter is followed by more than 40 practical recipes, all nutritionally analyzed, which will help you to achieve and maintain a healthy lifestyle. The recipes are delicious, suitable for all the family, and easy to prepare and cook. There are dishes that will satisfy the heartiest of appetites as well as stimulating a jaded palate. The food in this book is tempting and appealing, a far cry from the tired, limp salads, sad-looking vegetables, and brown-colored meals, which many people associate with healthy food.

Diet alone, however, is not the answer: exercise also plays an important part in the pursuit of a healthy lifestyle, so try to make time for this. You'll find additional information on exercise and eating out. Exercise is not the preserve of the fit—everyone can do it, so don't be put off. If you are starting from scratch, the secret is to do it gradually.

So be kind to yourself and your family and serve them food that not only will keep them fit and healthy—but that they will also love. Eat your way to good health!

1

nutrition and lifestyle

The Glycemic Index and a healthy diet

The Glycemic Index

The Glycemic Index (GI) is a system whereby ingredients and dishes are rated according to the rate at which a carbohydrate food breaks down into simple sugars and enters the bloodstream—we should be aiming for a slow, steady release for good blood sugar balance (see page 14). A low-GI diet can be extremely useful not only for people wanting to control their blood sugar levels but also for those wanting to lose weight, reduce the risk of heart disease, and boost their energy levels.

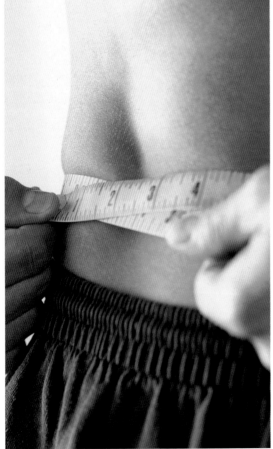

A GI diet is not only extremely healthy, it can also be great for losing weight.

What are the benefits of a low-GI diet?

• Low GI means a smaller rise in blood sugar levels after meals.
• Low GI foods tend to contain more fiber, so keep you feeling fuller for longer.
• Low GI can help you lose weight, as it promotes the use of fat over carbohydrate and protein for fuel by the body.
• Low GI can improve blood sugar control.
• Low GI can prolong physical endurance.
• Low GI can make you feel less tired and lethargic.

It is important to note that a low-GI diet, like any diet, needs to be balanced. No single food contains all the nutrients that you need, as different foods are rich in a range of nutrients. In order to achieve a healthy, balanced diet, you need to eat a variety of different foods every day, paying particular attention to both the quantity and the type of food chosen.

How can you achieve a healthy diet?

• Eat a variety of different foods from each food group.
• Eat regularly, never miss a meal.
• Choose high-fiber, whole-wheat products.
• Eat more fruit and vegetables, at least five portions a day.
• Choose healthy sources of fats such as avocados, olive oil, raw nuts and seeds, oily fish, and some lean white meat, rather than red meat and dairy products.
• Choose lean meat, fish, poultry, beans, and vegetarian alternatives instead of fatty meats or meat products.
• Eat oily fish two to three times a week.

If you follow these general guidelines, your body will be getting all the essential nutrients—carbohydrates, fat, protein, fiber, vitamins, and minerals—that it needs on a daily basis.

What affects GI value?

- Cooking—when you heat starchy foods up, they will be digested more easily.
- Processing—processed foods are more refined and so make the starches they contain faster to digest.
- Fat and protein—foods high in protein and fat are emptied more slowly from your stomach. They take longer to digest and so slow the breakdown and sugar release from carbohydrate foods.
- Acid—by adding an acidic food to your meal, the GI value will be lowered so it takes longer for your stomach to digest: eg, dressing added to a salad.

How can you achieve a low-GI diet?

Including a low-GI food with each meal or snack will lower the overall effect of your blood sugar levels and make them more stable. By doing so, you will feel less hungry in between meals and have more energy. You need to choose fewer processed foods and more high-fiber foods.

Achieving a low-GI diet

Breakfast

- Choose oat-based breakfast cereals.
- Add fruit and raw nuts to cereals.
- Have fresh fruit rather than juice.
- Eat "grainy" breads made with whole seeds.

Lunch

- Eat plenty of salads.
- Choose chunky bean or vegetable soups.
- Add variety with different types of breads, eg, multigrain, pumpernickel.

Evening meal

- Use brown basmati rice, bulgur wheat, or pearl barley.
- Include plenty of beans and lentils.
- Eat plenty of vegetables.
- Reduce the amount of potatoes you eat.

Desserts

- Try more fruit-based desserts.
- Add nuts to desserts

Glycemic Index ratings for some common foods

The Glycemic Index rates carbohydrate foods from 0 to 100 and measures the rise in blood sugar levels caused by a particular food, whether it be a dramatic rise, moderate, or low. Carbohydrate foods are those that contain glucose, which is found in plant foods. Cheese, eggs, fish, and meat contain only fat and protein and so cannot be included in the table.

The rating is determined by giving enough of a particular food to provide 50 g of carbohydrate and then measuring what effect this has on blood sugar levels. All foods are compared to the effect pure glucose has on blood glucose—which is given as an arbitrary figure of 100. You should aim for a range of low-GI foods in your diet.

Foods are given a score out of 100 and are classified as follows:

Foods that are quickly absorbed	**GI**	more than 70
Foods that take a moderate amount of time to be absorbed	**GI**	value 55–70
Foods that take longer to be absorbed	**GI**	less than 55

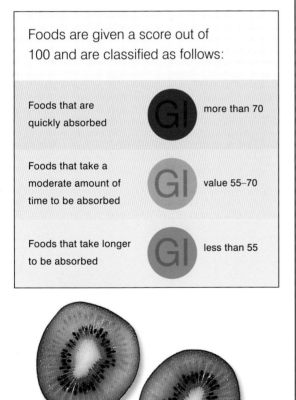

GI Low Foods

Fruit and Fruit Juices

Tomatoes	(15)
Cherries	(22)
Grapefruit	(25)
Dried apricots	(31)
Pears	(37)
Apples	(38)
Plums	(39)
Strawberries	(40)
Apple juice	(41)
Peaches	(42)
Oranges	(44)
Grapes	(46)
Pineapple juice	(46)
Grapefruit juice	(48)
Orange juice	(52)
Kiwifruit	(53)
Bananas	(54)

Vegetables

Broccoli	(10)
Cabbage	(10)
Lettuce	(10)
Mushrooms	(10)
Raw onions	(10)
Raw red bell peppers	(10)
Green peas	(48)
Raw carrots	(49)
Sweet potatoes	(54)

Grains

Pearl barley	(31)
Rye	(34)
Brown basmati rice	(52)

Breads

Mixed grain bread	(48)
German rye bread	(50)

Pasta

Vermicelli	(35)
Linguine	(42)
Instant noodles	(47)

Bakery Products

Sponge cake (with egg)	(46)

Breakfast Cereals

Bran cereal	(42)

Dairy

Lowfat plain yogurt	(14)
Whole milk	(27)
Skim milk	(27)
Lowfat fruit yogurt	(33)
Custard	(43)

Legumes

Soybeans	(14)
Red split lentils	(18)
Green lentils	(29)
Canned chickpeas	(42)
Canned pinto beans	(45)
Canned baked beans	(48)
Green peas	(48)

GI Medium Foods

Fruit
Mangoes	(56)
Golden raisins	(56)
Apricots	(57)
Raisins	(64)
Pineapple	(66)

Vegetables
Corn	(55)
New potatoes	(57)
Beet	(64)
Boiled/mashed potatoes	(70)

Grains
Buckwheat	(55)
Brown rice	(55)
White basmati rice	(58)

Breads
White pita bread	(58)
Hamburger buns	(61)
Rye flour bread	(64)
High-fiber wheat bread	(68)
Whole-wheat bread	(69)

Pasta
Durum wheat spaghetti	(55)

Bakery Products
Pastry	(59)
Muffins	(62)
Croissants	(67)
Crumpets	(69)

Breakfast Cereals
Granola	(56)
Porridge	(61)
Whole-wheat shredded biscuits	(69)
Wheat biscuits	(70)

Cookies
Oatmeal	(55)
Rich tea	(55)
Digestives	(59)
Shortbread	(64)

Savory Cookies and Crackers
Wheat thins	(67)

Dairy
Ice cream	(61)

Sugars
High-fruit preserve	(55)
Honey	(58)
White granulated sugar	(64)

Candies and Snacks
Popcorn	(55)

Beverages
Orange cordial	(66)
Fizzy orange	(68)

GI High Foods

Fruit
Watermelon	(72)

Vegetables
Rutabaga	(72)
French fries	(75)
Pumpkin	(75)
Baked potato	(85)
Cooked carrots	(85)
Parsnips	(97)

Grains
White rice	(88)

Breads
White bagels	(72)
White wheat bread	(78)
Gluten-free bread	(90)
French baguette	(95)

Bakery Products
Doughnuts	(76)
Waffles	(76)

Breakfast Cereals
Bran flakes with dried fruit	(71)
Puffed wheat	(74)
Crisped rice	(82)
Corn flakes	(83)

Savory Cookies and Crackers
Water biscuits	(71)
Rice cakes	(77)
Puffed crispbread	(81)

Legumes
Fava beans	(79)

Candies and Snacks
Corn tortillas	(74)
Jelly beans	(80)
Pretzels	(81)
Dates	(99)

Beverages
High-glucose sports drinks	(95)

Carbohydrates

Carbohydrates are plant foods (except lactose in milk) and found in a variety of sources. Their primary role is to provide your body with energy, so about 50 percent of your total daily calories should come from carbohydrates. Carbohydrates are broken down by your digestive system into glucose and transported along your bloodstream to parts of the body needing energy—such as your muscles and brain.

Carbohydrates are either "simple" (sugars) or "complex" (starches). You should limit your intake of sugars and get most of your energy requirements from starches.

Simple carbohydrates or sugars are found in processed foods, candies, cakes, sodas, fruit juices, and very refined carbohydrates, such as white bread, where the bran part of the wheat has been stripped away.

Complex carbohydrates release their sugars more slowly and are termed *starches*. They also contain *fiber* that helps to slow down sugar release and take toxins out of the body to help prevent disease. Vegetables, nuts, pulses, whole grains, and fruits in their raw, natural state provide complex carbohydrates bound in fiber. They therefore take much more time to breakdown into their simple sugars and provide a more slow and steady release into the bloodstream.

The importance of exercise

Regular exercise is an essential part of a healthy lifestyle. If you want to reduce your risk of developing disease, increase your life expectancy, and improve your quality of life when you are old, then you need to stay active. Half the battle with exercise is motivating yourself to start and then keeping it up on a regular basis, but there are plenty of good reasons to keep you going. Both your body and your mind will reap tremendous benefits from physical activity.

The physical benefits of exercise

Exercise protects your physical health and has many positive effects on how your body works—your heart muscles become stronger and pump more blood more quickly around your body to pick up fatty deposits and waste products. As a result, blood pressure and cholesterol levels are lowered, reducing your risk of developing heart disease or stroke. Your lungs become stronger and your body more efficient in the way in which it uses oxygen. Bones stay strong and healthy, muscles become stronger, and joint mobility and stability will improve, helping to keep you independent and active in later life. As you age, your metabolism (the rate at which your body uses energy) slows down and your body needs fewer calories, but if you remain active you will avoid excess weight gain in old age because physical activity boosts your metabolic rate.

How exercise benefits your mind

Regular exercise can improve your psychological well-being. When you exercise, your brain releases morphine-like chemicals called endorphins that act as natural antidepressants to make you feel relaxed and in a good mood. The feeling of well-being that follows exercise will reduce any stress and tension. By exercising regularly you are more likely to feel and look healthy, which will increase your confidence and self-esteem.

The other nutrients

Fats

Fat has had a bad press. We need fat in the diet for resistance to infection, hormone function, cholesterol regulation, healthy cell membranes, and optimum mental function. It is important to adopt a healthy attitude to fats and realize that they are not all bad and that we are made up of a large proportion of fat —they make up more than 60 percent of your brain and need to be continually replenished for good mental function, concentration, memory, and mood.

Fats are crucial in your diet to ensure that you obtain all the nutrients you need on a daily basis. They provide essential fatty acids and are carriers for certain vitamins. You do not have to cut out fats completely in your diet to lose weight—what is important is to look at how much fat you eat. Fat provides energy—1 gram provides 9 kcals, so if a food contains a lot of fat it means that it also provides you with a lot of calories. For example, an average serving of butter on toast contains 9 grams fat, which provides 81 kcals, so if you swapped this for a lowfat margarine you would have 3.6 grams of fat and 32 kcals.

Fats are made up of fatty acids and glycerol and are divided into saturated or unsaturated. It is recommended that no more than 35 percent of your total daily calories should come from fats, 10 percent being from saturated fats. This means that if your calorie intake was 2000 kcals per day only 35 percent should be from fats. As each gram of fat provides 9 kcals, your total daily intake of should be no more than 77.8 g fat—that's just over 3 oz.

SATURATED FATS are the fats that you should reduce in your diet, as high intakes can lead to an increase in your blood cholesterol levels, which in turn increases the risk of coronary heart disease. Main sources in your diet are dairy foods including butter, cheese, cream, milk, fatty meats, and lard. As a rule of thumb, saturated fats tend to be a solid at room

A balance of unsaturated fats is essential for a healthy diet.

temperature and are derived from animal sources. However, there are some exceptions—coconut and palm oil, plus some margarines and oils labeled "hydrogenated." The latter should be avoided in your diet because during processing some of their unsaturated fats are changed to saturated fats.

UNSATURATED FATS can be divided into two types—polyunsaturated and monounsaturated. There are two types of polyunsaturated fats, Omega 3 and Omega 6. Omega 3 are from oily, coldwater fish such as mackerel, herring, salmon, tuna, trout, sardines, and anchovies. However, these can contain high levels of mercury or other toxins, so it is best to limit your intake to about three times a week. The smaller the fish, the less mercury it will have accumulated. The best vegetarian sources are flax (linseed), hemp, and pumpkin (pepitas) seeds and their cold-pressed oils. Omega 6 are of vegetable or plant origin, including hemp seed, Evening Primrose Oil, borage, sunflower seeds, pumpkin (pepitas) seeds, and sesame seeds and their oils. Nuts, except peanuts, are also good sources. Polyunsaturated fats tend to be liquid at room temperature and it is essential to include them in your diet, as they can help to reduce blood cholesterol levels and maintain good health.

Monounsaturated fats are considered to protect against heart disease because they can help to reduce your blood cholesterol levels. They can be found in foods like olive oil, canola oil, avocados, peanuts, almonds, and oily fish.

Protein

Protein is found in meat, fish, eggs, and dairy products as well as beans, peas, lentils, and other vegetarian alternatives. Its main purpose is to provide building blocks for growth and maintenance of your muscles and tissues, so 10–15 percent of your total daily calories should come from protein. If your diet is varied and balanced, containing some protein at each meal, you should be able to meet your daily protein requirements. Overly high intakes can lead to health problems such as kidney diseases.

Protein is made up of amino acids—there are 20 naturally occurring and protein foods contain varying amounts of each. Your body is also able to make up some amino acids from your diet, but there are eight that it cannot make. These are known as essential amino acids and must be obtained from your diet.

Once eaten, protein is broken down into amino acids and absorbed in the small intestine. The acids are then transported to the liver for processing and released into your bloodstream to make up enzymes, hormones, body cells, hair, nails, bones, muscles, and DNA. Your body is always recombining amino acids to make new cells and nearly all your body cells are able to make specific protein for their needs.

Fiber

Fiber is a form of carbohydrate that we do not use for fuel. Also called nonstarch polysaccharide, it is simply the skeleton part of plants. It is found mainly in the outer walls of plants and seeds.

Fiber passes through your digestive system rather than being digested and absorbed into the body. You should aim for 18 g of fiber a day, so it is important that you include a variety of high-fiber foods each day in your diet. There are two types of fiber in your diet, each with a different role:

Insoluble fiber is found in wheat bran, whole-grain bread and cereals, and fruit and vegetables. It helps maintain a healthy digestive system, as it holds water and increases bulk, which stimulates the muscles of your digestive system. This means that the muscles in your digestive system are kept healthy and toned, helping to prevent constipation, hemorrhoids, and bowel cancer.

Soluble fiber, found in oats, beans, dried or canned pulses, and fruit and vegetables, plays a role in lowering blood cholesterol.

Be warned—if you increase your fiber intake to ensure a healthy, balanced diet, you must also drink plenty of fluids, at least 8–10 glasses a day.

Cheese, a source of protein, can be beneficial for a balanced diet.

Eating a range of fruits can supply soluble and insoluble fiber.

Vitamins and minerals

Most people are able to meet their daily requirements for vitamins and minerals by eating a varied diet. At times some people may have higher requirements—eg during illness, later life, when pregnant or on certain medication—and they will need to ensure that they eat foods rich in certain vitamins and minerals. They could also be advised to take supplements to compensate.

Vitamins are needed to carry out many processes in your body and are grouped into two categories: fat soluble (vitamins A, D, E, and K) and water soluble (vitamins C, B_1, B_2, B_5, B_6, B_{12}, niacin, biotin, and folic acid). Vitamins are susceptible to damage by heat, light, oxygen, enzymes, and minerals, and losses can occur during food processing, preparation, and storage. All nutrients work together in synergy for body functions.

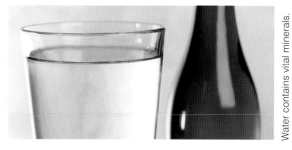

Water contains vital minerals.

Minerals are needed in larger amounts than vitamins, for a variety of functions in your body. Absorption of minerals can be influenced by a variety of factors:
• Iron absorption is increased when vitamin C is eaten at the same meal.
• Zinc absorption is reduced when there is an excess intake of iron.
• Iodine absorption is reduced by nitrates.
• Phytates and oxalates hinder the absorption of calcium, iron, and zinc.

Eating out and entertaining

For most people, the hardest part of weight control is not dieting but keeping the weight off permanently. Long-term weight management doesn't mean you can't entertain, go out, or take part in the Christmas festivities. Here are some ideas to help you keep in control of what's on your plate.

Anticipate If you know you're entertaining or going out to dinner, try eating very healthily the day before and plan to fit in some exercise to compensate, even if it's just a long walk the day after. It also helps to think about what you might order before you go out so that you can choose the healthiest options on the menu and not be tempted to try everything on the cheeseboard.

Keep it plain Choose food that is cooked simply and not drowned in high-calorie sauces—broiled fish and meat are good options.

Say no to the extras Stick to what you've ordered and avoid the extra calories lurking in the bread and olive oil, the poppadams and chutneys, the nachos and cheese.

Skip the appetizer or dessert Limit yourself to two courses and save calories.

Buffet management When serving yourself at a buffet, try limiting yourself to two or three types of food on your plate at a time. Start with the low-calorie options—the vegetables and salads—to leave less room for more fattening foods.

How to deal with alcohol Alcohol is an appetite stimulant and because it relaxes your inhibitions you are more likely to be careless over what you eat. Never drink on an empty stomach—if you know you're going out drinking, eat something light beforehand. Always start off with a soda or water, and match every alcoholic drink with a nonalcoholic one.

2

breakfasts and brunches

Summer Smoothie

5 minutes

no cooking required

GI low

Smoothies provide a quick, healthy, and delicious drink that's both filling and nutritious—ideal when there is no time to sit and eat or as a refreshing early morning appetizer.

SERVES 2

generous $3/4$ cup strawberries

generous $3/4$ cup raspberries

$3/8$ cup blueberries

1 ripe passion fruit

$2/3$ cup lowfat milk

TO DECORATE

2 scoops frozen strawberry yogurt
or 1 tbsp crushed ice and 2 tbsp
strained plain yogurt

2 strawberries

1 Lightly rinse the strawberries, raspberries, and blueberries, and scoop out the passion fruit pulp. Place all the fruits in a juicer or blender and blend for 1 minute. Add the milk and blend again.

2 Either pour into tall glasses and top with the yogurt or place some crushed ice in glasses, then pour in the fruit juice and place the scoops of yogurt on top. Decorate with the strawberries.

Serving Analysis			
Energy (kcals)	68	Protein (grams)	4.3
Total fat (grams)	1.5	Carbohydrate (grams)	11.6
of which saturated fat (grams)	0.2	of which sugars (grams)	11.6
Fat/100 g product (grams)	**0.5**		

Toasted Granola

10 minutes

10–12 minutes

GI low

This delicious crunchy granola can be eaten on its own with a little skim or lowfat milk or sprinkled over grapefruit segments or melon chunks with strawberries.

SERVES 4

2²⁄₃ **cups jumbo Scotch oats**

¹⁄₂ **cup dried apricots, coarsely chopped**

generous ¹⁄₃ **cup raisins**

scant ¹⁄₄ **cup dried cranberries**

¹⁄₂ **cup wheat bran**

TO SERVE

skim milk

fresh fruit, such as sliced banana, strawberries, and blueberries

Cook's Tip

Make the granola ahead of time and store in an airtight container, then use as required.

1 Preheat the oven to 400°F/200°C. Pour the Scotch oats into a shallow dish. Cook in the oven for 10–12 minutes, or until the oats are golden. Stir the oats occasionally. Remove and let cool, then place in a bowl.

2 Add the raisins, apricots, cranberries, and wheat bran and place in an airtight container. Serve 3–4 tablespoons of the granola in bowls with skim milk and top with fresh fruit.

Serving Analysis			
Energy (kcals)	129	Protein (grams)	4.3
Total fat (grams)	2.3	Carbohydrate (grams)	23
of which saturated fat (grams)	0.4	of which sugars (grams)	5.1
Fat/100 g product (grams)	**0.05**		

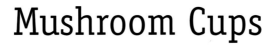

Mushroom Cups

12 minutes

23 minutes

GI low

Large portobello mushrooms can be served with a variety of fillings, such as roasted vegetables, three-bean salad, or stir-fried bell peppers and onion.

SERVES 4

2 red bell peppers, seeded and cut into quarters

4–8 portobello mushrooms, depending on size

1–2 tsp extra virgin olive oil

3 oz/85 g green beans, trimmed

1 egg

2 egg whites

2 tbsp skim milk

1 tbsp chopped fresh flat-leaf parsley

salt and pepper

broiled tomatoes, to serve (optional)

Cook's Tip

If liked, add 2 chopped tomatoes or some chopped cooked asparagus to the scrambled eggs once cooked, or coarsely chop 2 oz/55 g white mushrooms and cook with the eggs.

1 Preheat the broiler and line the broiler rack with foil. Place the red bell pepper under the broiler and cook for 5–8 minutes, or until the skins are charred. Turn the peppers occasionally so they are evenly charred. Transfer the peppers to a plastic bag and let cool. When cool enough to handle, remove the skin.

2 Wipe the mushrooms, then remove and discard the stalks. Heat the oil in a skillet and very gently sauté the mushrooms for 4–5 minutes, or until lightly cooked. (Cover the skillet with a lid to help with the cooking process.)

3 Meanwhile, cook the green beans in lightly boiling water for 4 minutes, then drain and keep warm.

4 To make the scrambled egg filling, beat the egg with the egg whites, milk, and seasoning to taste. Stir in the parsley. Heat a small nonstick skillet, then pour in the egg mixture. Cook, stirring occasionally, over medium heat for 4–5 minutes, or until lightly set.

5 Place 2 bell pepper quarters and beans on warmed serving plates, then fill the mushroom cups with the scrambled egg mixture. Place on top of the beans. Serve with broiled tomatoes if liked.

Serving Analysis			
Energy (kcals)	58	Protein (grams)	4.9
Total fat (grams)	2.8	Carbohydrate (grams)	3.4
of which saturated fat (grams)	0.7	of which sugars (grams)	3
Fat/100 g product (grams)	2		

Date and Banana Muffins

- 15 minutes
- 10–20 minutes
- **GI** medium

It is not a good idea to skip breakfast, so if you are in a rush, take a muffin with you—it will keep you going through the morning, thus avoiding the need to nibble. For low-GI muffins, replace the dates with apricots.

SERVES 6–12

1½ cups self-rising whole-wheat flour

1 tsp baking powder

1 tsp ground cinnamon

½ cup wheat bran

⅛ cup packed brown sugar

generous ⅜ cup chopped dates

1 ripe banana, peeled and mashed

1 egg, beaten

2 egg whites

up to ⅔ cup orange juice

Cook's Tip

Muffins are always best eaten warm, so make these ahead of time and either reheat for 30–40 seconds in a microwave or in a conventional oven for about 5 minutes.

1 Preheat the oven to 350°F/180°C. Place 6 paper muffin cases into a muffin pan or 12 paper baking cases into a bun pan. Sift the flour, baking powder, and ground cinnamon into a mixing bowl, then tip in the bran residue that is left in the strainer plus the ½ cup of bran.

2 Stir in the sugar, dates, and mashed banana. Add the egg and egg whites, then mix in enough orange juice to give a soft dropping consistency. Spoon into the paper cases.

3 Bake in the oven for 10–20 minutes, or until risen and the tops spring back when touched lightly with a clean finger. Remove and serve warm.

Serving Analysis			
Energy (kcals)	205	Protein (grams)	8.1
Total fat (grams)	2.2	Carbohydrate (grams)	41.1
of which saturated fat (grams)	0.5	of which sugars (grams)	16.4
Fat/100 g product (grams)	1.9		

5 minutes

8–10 minutes

GI low

Oatmeal with Fruit

This recipe can be made the evening before and left refrigerated overnight, or made in the morning and eaten immediately. It is perfect to sustain the whole family throughout the morning.

SERVES 4

2 cups jumbo Scotch oats

$^5/_8$ cup oatmeal

pinch of salt (optional)

$3^1/_2$ cups skim milk

$^1/_3$ cup dried apricots, chopped

$^1/_8$ cup sunflower seeds

sliced banana, to serve

1 Place the oats and oatmeal in a pan together with the salt, if using, and stir in the milk. Place over gentle heat and cook, stirring, for 7–8 minutes, or until the oats thicken.

2 Stir the apricots and sunflower seeds into the porridge, then spoon into individual dishes and top with the sliced banana. Alternatively, place the porridge in the dishes and top with the fruits and seeds.

Cook's Tip

If you want to make the porridge the evening before, place the oats, oatmeal, salt, and milk into the top of a double boiler and cook over gently simmering water for about 25–30 minutes, or until thickened. Remove from the heat. The following day reheat the porridge gently, stirring occasionally, and serve topped with the fruit and seeds.

Serving Analysis			
Energy (kcals)	164	Protein (grams)	7.8
Total fat (grams)	3.5	Carbohydrate (grams)	26.5
of which saturated fat (grams)	0.5	of which sugars (grams)	7.9
Fat/100 g product (grams)	**2.4**		

12 minutes

12 minutes

GI low

Smoked Salmon with Broccoli

This dish is an ideal choice for brunch, together with Date and Banana Muffins and a Midsummer Smoothie.

SERVES 4

8 oz/225 g broccoli

4 eggs

2 tsp lemon juice (optional)

8 oz/225 g smoked salmon

whole-wheat bread, to serve

DRESSING

²/₃ cup lowfat cream cheese

1–1½ tsp Dijon mustard

2 tsp snipped fresh chives

Cook's Tip

Place dough cutters in the water and poach the eggs in them so they keep their shape.

1 Divide the broccoli into spears, then cook in boiling water for 5–6 minutes, or until tender. Drain and keep warm while you poach the eggs.

2 To poach the eggs, half-fill a large skillet with water, then add the lemon juice, if using, and bring to a boil. Reduce the heat to a simmer, then carefully break 1 egg into a cup and slip into the simmering water. Repeat with the remaining eggs. Poach the eggs for 4–5 minutes, or until set to personal preference.

3 Meanwhile, divide the smoked salmon between 4 individual plates. Stir all the dressing ingredients together in a mixing cup until blended.

4 Place the broccoli spears on the plates and top each with a poached egg, then spoon over a little dressing and serve. Serve with whole-wheat bread.

Serving Analysis			
Energy (kcals)	143	Protein (grams)	20.7
Total fat (grams)	3.6	Carbohydrate (grams)	7.4
of which saturated fat (grams)	0.8	of which sugars (grams)	7.2
Fat/100 g product (grams)	1.2		

Vegetable Pancakes

20 minutes

12 minutes

GI low

Quick and easy to prepare and cook, Vegetable Rösti is ideal to serve both as a main component of breakfast or brunch or as an accompaniment to a main meal.

SERVES 4

1 carrot, grated

1 zucchini, grated

1 sweet potato, grated

8 scallions, finely chopped or shredded

1 egg white, beaten

2 tsp extra virgin olive oil

pepper

8 lean Canadian bacon slices, to serve (optional)

1 Mix all the vegetables together and season with pepper to taste, then stir in the egg white. Using clean hands, form into 8 small patties. Press them firmly together.

2 Heat the oil in a nonstick skillet and cook the patties over gentle heat for 5–6 minutes, or until golden. Turn over halfway through the cooking time and press down with the back of a spatula. Do this in 2 batches to prevent the skillet from being overcrowded.

3 Meanwhile, preheat the broiler and line the broiler rack with foil. Place the bacon under the broiler and cook for 5-8 minutes, until crisp, or cook to personal preference. Turn the slices over halfway through the cooking time.

4 As soon as the patties and bacon are cooked, serve immediately.

Cook's Tip

If liked, cook as 1 large rösti. Place all the mixture in the heated skillet and press down with a spatula. Cook for 6–8 minutes, then invert onto a large plate and slip the mixture back into the skillet. Cook for another 4–6 minutes.

Serving Analysis			
Energy (kcals)	85	Protein (grams)	3.3
Total fat (grams)	3.5	Carbohydrate (grams)	10.8
of which saturated fat (grams)	0.8	of which sugars (grams)	5.2
Fat/100 g product (grams)	**2.7**		

15 minutes

40 minutes

GI low

Saffron-Flavored Fish

You can vary the fish used here according to personal preference. Smoked or fresh salmon, trout, or even shrimp would work well.

SERVES 4

generous ½ cup brown basmati rice

1 tsp extra virgin olive oil

1 onion, cut into small wedges

1–2 red fresh chilies, to taste, seeded and chopped

few saffron strands

½–1 tsp ground coriander

3 cups vegetable or fish stock

1 lb/450 g white fish fillet, such as cod or haddock

4 oz/115 g broccoli

8 oz/225 g cherry tomatoes, halved

4–6 scallions, trimmed and chopped

pepper

1 tbsp chopped fresh cilantro

Cook's Tip

Covering the skillet with a lid or a large piece of foil helps to keep the moisture in and also speeds up the cooking process.

1 Rinse the rice and shake off any excess water. Heat the oil in a large skillet, then add the rice, onion, and chilies and cook over medium heat, stirring, for 2 minutes. Add the saffron strands and ground coriander and cook for an additional 1 minute before pouring in half of the stock. Bring to a boil, then reduce the heat to a simmer and cover. Cook for 15 minutes, stirring occasionally and adding more stock as necessary so that the rice does not dry out.

2 Meanwhile, skin the fish and remove any pin bones, then rinse and cut into small pieces. Set aside. Divide the broccoli into tiny florets and cook in lightly boiling water for 5 minutes. Drain and keep warm. Add the fish to the rice and cook for an additional 5 minutes.

3 Add the tomatoes and broccoli to the rice and fish mixture and cook for another 5 minutes before adding the scallions, pepper to taste, and cilantro. Cook for 2–3 minutes, or until the rice is tender but retains a bite. Serve immediately.

Serving Analysis			
Energy (kcals)	239	Protein (grams)	26.2
Total fat (grams)	2.8	Carbohydrate (grams)	27.1
of which saturated fat (grams)	0.3	of which sugars (grams)	3.5
Fat/100 g product (grams)	**1.1**		

34   Breakfasts and Brunches

ight snacks and appetizers

Spicy Hummus

5 minutes

no cooking required

GI low

This dip can be served on many different occasions, as an appetizer, light lunch, or even as an accompaniment to a main meal in place of rice, potato, or pasta.

SERVES 6

14 oz/400 g canned chickpeas, drained and rinsed

2–4 garlic cloves, peeled and crushed

1 fresh red chili, seeded and chopped

2 tbsp sesame seed paste

4 tbsp lime juice

2–4 tbsp cooled boiled water

1 tbsp chopped cilantro

pepper

CRUDITES

2 carrots, peeled and cut into sticks

1 red bell pepper, seeded and cut into strips

1/2 cucumber, peeled if preferred and cut into strips

4 celery stalks, trimmed and cut into small strips

Cook's tip

If using dried chickpeas, rinse thoroughly and soak overnight. The following day, drain, then place in a pan and cover with water. Bring to a boil, then discard the water. Cover with fresh water and bring to a boil, then let simmer for 1 hour, or until tender. Drain and proceed as above.

1 Place the chickpeas, garlic, and chili in a food processor and blend for 1 minute or until finely chopped. Add the sesame seed paste and blend again for 30 seconds.

2 With the motor still running, gradually pour in the lime juice and then enough water to give a soft dipping consistency.

3 Add pepper to taste and the chopped cilantro and blend for an additional 1 minute. Scrape into a small bowl and serve with Crudités.

Serving Analysis

Energy (kcals)	138	Protein (grams)	6.9
Total fat (grams)	5.2	Carbohydrate (grams)	16.8
of which saturated fat (grams)	0.7	of which sugars (grams)	5.3
Fat/100 g product (grams)	**2.7**		

10 mins, plus 30
minutes' soaking

no cooking required

GI low

Tomato and Olive Dip

This dip is ideal to serve with a salad instead of a dressing or mayonnaise or as an alternative sauce to accompany the Thai-Style Fish Cakes.

Cook's tip

If using sun-dried tomatoes in oil, drain off the oil thoroughly, rinse, and pat dry before use.

SERVES 6

1 tbsp sun-dried tomatoes

generous ⅛ cup black olives, pitted

1 tsp tomato paste

1⅛ cups Quark

2 tbsp orange or lemon juice

pinch of paprika

pepper

Crudités, to serve

CRUDITES

2 carrots, peeled and cut into sticks

1 red bell pepper, seeded and cut into strips

½ cucumber, peeled if preferred and cut into strips

4 celery stalks, trimmed and cut into small strips

1 Chop the sun-dried tomatoes and place in a bowl, then cover with almost boiling water. Let stand for 30 minutes.

2 Place the tomatoes with 2 tablespoons of their soaking liquid in a food processor and blend for 1 minute. Add the olives and process to form a paste, adding more of the soaking liquid if required. Add the Quark and using the pulse button, blend to form a soft consistency, adding the orange or lemon juice at the end.

3 Add pepper to taste and blend for an additional 20 seconds. Scrape the dip into a small bowl and sprinkle over a little paprika. Serve with Crudités.

Serving Analysis			
Energy (kcals)	69	Protein (grams)	6.9
Total fat (grams)	1.9	Carbohydrate (grams)	6.2
of which saturated fat (grams)	0.3	of which sugars (grams)	5.9
Fat/100 g product (grams)	1.3		

15 minutes, plus 20 minutes' soaking

20 minutes

GI low

Bell Pepper and Mushroom Sauté

Bell peppers bring a lot of color to a dish, but they have a reputation for being slightly indigestible. Removing the skins reduces this problem a little. Use either peeled or not, as you prefer.

SERVES 4

1/4 oz/10 g dried porcini mushrooms (cèpes)

2 tsp extra virgin olive oil

1 onion, cut into small wedges

2–4 garlic cloves, sliced

4 oz/115 g lean Canadian bacon, fat discarded

1 red bell pepper, seeded and cut into strips

1 yellow bell pepper, seeded and cut into strips

1 orange bell pepper, seeded and cut into strips

2/3 cup vegetable stock or red wine

1–2 tbsp shredded fresh basil

pepper

freshly cooked baby new potatoes, to serve (optional)

1 Pick over the mushrooms and place in a small bowl. Cover with hot, not boiling, water and leave for 20 minutes. Drain, reserving the soaking liquid, and set aside.

2 Heat the oil in a large skillet and add the onion and garlic, then cook over medium heat for 3 minutes, stirring occasionally.

3 Cut the bacon into strips, then add to the skillet and cook for 2 minutes. Add the drained mushrooms with their soaking liquor and the bell peppers and sauté for 5 minutes, stirring occasionally.

4 Pour in the stock and bring to a boil, then reduce the heat to a simmer and cook for 8–10 minutes, or until the bell peppers are soft but still retain a bite.

5 Season with pepper to taste and sprinkle with the shredded basil, and serve with cooked baby new potatoes, also sprinkled with shredded basil.

Cook's Tip

If you want to peel the bell peppers, cut each bell pepper into quarters and discard the seeds and membrane. Place on a foil-lined broiler rack. Cook under a preheated hot broiler for 5–8 minutes, turning the peppers round as the skins blacken. Let cool in a plastic bag for about 10 minutes, or until cool enough to handle. The skins can then easily be peeled off.

Serving Analysis

Energy (kcals)	130	Protein (grams)	7.7
Total fat (grams)	3.9	Carbohydrate (grams)	10.1
of which saturated fat (grams)	1	of which sugars (grams)	8
Fat/100 g product (grams)	**1.8**		

Sweet Potato Blinis

20 minutes

45 minutes

GI low

These blinis are very versatile. Try them for an informal lunch, or as and unusual dinner party appetizer, or make them smaller and serve as canapés.

SERVES 4–6

4 oz/115 g sweet potatoes, peeled and cut into chunks

1 tsp ground allspice

generous 1/3 cup whole wheat flour

1 egg

2/3 cup skim milk

1 egg white

pepper

FILLING

3 oz/85 g prosciutto, fat discarded

3 tomatoes, thickly sliced

2/3 cup lowfat cream cheese

1 tbsp finely grated lemon rind

1 tbsp chopped fresh parsley

1 oz/25 g arugula leaves

Cook's Tip

Keep the blinis warm, either covered with foil in a warm oven or wrapped in a clean dish towel on a plate set over a pan of gently simmering water.

1 Cook the sweet potatoes in boiling water over medium heat for 15 minutes, or until soft. Drain and mash until smooth, then season with pepper to taste and stir in the ground allspice and flour. Place in a mixing bowl.

2 Add the whole egg and beat it into the mashed sweet potatoes, then gradually stir in the milk to give a thick batter consistency. Set aside until required.

3 Prepare the filling. Preheat the broiler. Cut the prosciutto into strips. Place the tomatoes on a foil-lined broiler rack and, just before serving, cook under the preheated hot broiler for 3–4 minutes, or until hot. Blend the cream cheese with the lemon rind and parsley. Set aside.

4 Whisk the egg white until stiff and stir it into the sweet potato batter. Heat a nonstick skillet until hot, then place 3–4 spoonfuls of the batter in the skillet and swirl to form a 3-inch/7.5-cm circle. Cook for 2–3 minutes, or until set, then turn over and cook for an additional 2–3 minutes, or until golden. Keep warm while you cook the remaining batter.

5 Place 2–3 blinis on a plate and top with a little arugula, prosciutto, and broiled tomato, then spoon over a little of the cream cheese and serve.

Serving Analysis

Energy (kcals)	116	Protein (grams)	9.5
Total fat (grams)	3.3	Carbohydrate (grams)	12.9
of which saturated fat (grams)	1	of which sugars (grams)	4.2
Fat/100 g product (grams)	**2.4**		

20 minutes

16 minutes

GI low

Thai-Style Fish Cakes

These fish cakes are extremely easy to make, and provide a tasty and delicious midweek snack. Try serving them with freshly cooked brown basmati rice and an Asian-style salad.

SERVES 6

14 oz/400 g canned white crabmeat

1–2 Thai chilies, to taste, seeded and finely chopped

6 scallions, finely shredded

1 zucchini, grated

1 carrot, grated

1 small yellow bell pepper, seeded and finely shredded

1/2 cup fresh bean sprouts, rinsed

1 tbsp chopped cilantro

1 large egg white

1–2 tbsp sunflower-seed or corn oil

SALSA

1 Thai chili, seeded and finely chopped

2-inch/5-cm piece cucumber, grated

1 tbsp chopped cilantro

1 tbsp lime juice

1 tbsp Thai sweet chili sauce

1 tbsp peanuts, finely chopped (optional)

TO SERVE

rice salad (optional)

salad (optional)

1 Mix all the fish cake ingredients, except for the egg white and oil, together. Whisk the egg white until frothy and just beginning to stiffen, then stir into the crab mixture. Then, using your hands, press about 1–2 tablespoons of the mixture together to form a fish cake. Repeat until 12 fish cakes are formed.

2 Make the salsa by combining all the ingredients except for the peanuts. Spoon into a small bowl, then cover and let stand for 30 minutes for the flavors to develop. Sprinkle with the peanuts, if using.

3 Heat 1 teaspoon of the oil in a nonstick skillet over low heat. Cook the fish cakes in batches for 2 minutes on each side over medium heat until lightly browned. Take care when turning them over. Remove and drain on paper towels. Repeat until all the fish cakes are cooked, using more oil if necessary. Serve with the salsa and with rice and salad, if liked.

Serving Analysis

Energy (kcals)	109	Protein (grams)	14.5
Total fat (grams)	3.7	Carbohydrate (grams)	4.5
of which saturated fat (grams)	0.5	of which sugars (grams)	3.9
Fat/100 g product (grams)	**2.2**		

8–10 minutes

12 minutes

GI low

Wild Mushroom Omelet

If fresh wild mushrooms are unavailable, look for dried porcini mushrooms (cèpes). Cover with warm water and soak for 20 minutes, then drain and use.

Cook's Tip

If liked, the omelet can be placed under a preheated hot broiler for the last 2 minutes of the cooking time in order to brown the cheese.

SERVES 2–4

1 tsp extra virgin olive oil

1 small onion, cut into wedges

2–3 garlic cloves, crushed

3 oz/85 g assorted wild mushrooms, cleaned and cut in half if large

1 zucchini, trimmed and grated

3 oz/85 g closed cup mushrooms, wiped and sliced

2 eggs plus 2 egg whites

1 yellow bell pepper, seeded, peeled, and cut into strips

1 tbsp freshly grated Parmesan cheese (optional)

1 tbsp shredded fresh basil

pepper

TO SERVE

tossed green salad

warm whole-wheat bread (optional)

1 Heat the oil in a large nonstick skillet and cook the onion and garlic over very gentle heat for 3 minutes. Cover the skillet during cooking. Stir occasionally. Add the mushrooms and cook for an additional 4–5 minutes, or until the mushrooms have softened slightly. Add the grated zucchini.

2 Beat the whole eggs with the egg whites, pepper to taste, and 2 tablespoons of water. Pour into the skillet and increase the heat slightly, then cook, drawing the egg into the center of the skillet from the edges with a fork or spatula.

3 When the omelet is set on the bottom, sprinkle the strips of yellow bell pepper over it, followed by the Parmesan cheese, if using, and basil. Cook for an additional 3–4 minutes, or until set to personal preference.

4 Serve the omelet cut into wedges with a tossed green salad, and, if liked, warm chunks of whole-wheat bread.

Serving Analysis			
Energy (kcals)	87	Protein (grams)	7.3
Total fat (grams)	4.4	Carbohydrate (grams)	4.8
of which saturated fat (grams)	1.1	of which sugars (grams)	3.5
Fat/100 g product (grams)	**2.5**		

Prosciutto with Melon and Asparagus

15 minutes

5 minutes

GI low

When eating melons, it is important that they are ripe, but not over- or underripe. When choosing a melon, a good indication is to gently press one end—it should yield slightly—and to smell it. Ripe melons will give off a sweet, pleasant aroma. Keep out of the refrigerator for best results.

SERVES 4

8 oz/225 g baby asparagus spears

1 small or ½ medium-size Galia or Canteloupe melon

2 oz/55 g prosciutto, thinly sliced

5½ oz/150 g bag of mixed salad greens, such as herb salad with arugula

⅝ cup fresh raspberries

1 tbsp freshly shaved Parmesan cheese

1 tbsp balsamic vinegar

2 tbsp orange juice

2 tbsp raspberry vinegar

1 Trim the asparagus, cutting in half if very long. Cook in lightly boiled water over medium heat for 5 minutes, or until tender. Drain and plunge into cold water, then drain again and set aside.

2 Cut the melon in half and scoop out the seeds. Cut into small wedges and cut away the rind. Separate the prosciutto and cut the slices in half, then wrap around the melon wedges.

3 Arrange the salad greens on a large serving platter and place the melon wedges on top together with the asparagus spears.

4 Scatter over the raspberries and Parmesan shavings. Place the vinegars and juice in a screw-top jar and shake until blended. Pour over the salad and serve.

Cook's Tip

To make raspberry vinegar, place 1¾ cups raspberries in a bowl and cover with 2½ cups of white wine vinegar. Cover and let stand for 24 hours, then strain, reserving the vinegar. Place another 1¾ cups of raspberries in a bowl and cover with the strained vinegar. Let stand for 24 hours, then strain and pour into clean sterilized jars. Screw down tightly and store in a cool dark place.

Serving Analysis

Energy (kcals)	95	Protein (grams)	7.8
Total fat (grams)	3.3	Carbohydrate (grams)	8.7
of which saturated fat (grams)	1.2	of which sugars (grams)	8.6
Fat/100 g product (grams)	**1.2**		

12 minutes

33 minutes

GI low

Barley and Vegetable Soup

Pearl barley seems to have fallen out of fashion, having been ousted by trendier ingredients. Here it is used not only to thicken the potage but also to add flavor.

Cook's Tip

Other green vegetables can be used if preferred: try shredded bok choy, kale, or baby spinach. Adjust the cooking time accordingly.

SERVES 4

1 tsp sunflower-seed or corn oil

1 onion, chopped

2 garlic cloves, crushed

1 carrot, diced

2 celery stalks, chopped

generous ¼ cup pearl barley, rinsed

5 cups vegetable stock

½ cup frozen peas

8 oz/225 g green cabbage, outer leaves and hard stalk discarded

pepper

1 Heat the oil in a large pan, then add the onion, garlic, carrot, and celery and cook over gentle heat for 5 minutes. Stir occasionally.

2 Sprinkle in the pearl barley and stir well. Pour in the stock and bring to a boil. Cover, then reduce the heat to a simmer and cook for 15 minutes. Add the peas and cook for an additional 5 minutes.

3 Wash the cabbage and shred finely. Add to the pan and cook for 2–3 minutes, or until the cabbage is just tender. Season with pepper to taste and serve immediately.

Serving Analysis

Energy (kcals)	133	Protein (grams)	8.1
Total fat (grams)	1.7	Carbohydrate (grams)	22.2
of which saturated fat (grams)	0.1	of which sugars (grams)	6.7
Fat/100 g product (grams)	**0.8**		

4

main courses

Chicken in Red Wine

10 minutes

30 minutes

GI low

Don't be tempted to use cheap wine in cooking, as it will have an adverse effect on the flavor of the dish. Good-quality food needs good-quality wine.

SERVES 4

4 skinless, boneless chicken breasts

1 tsp extra virgin olive oil

1 onion, cut into small wedges

2–3 garlic cloves, thinly sliced

1 red bell pepper, seeded and cut into thin strips

1¼ cups chicken stock

²/₃ cups red wine

1 tbsp black olives, pitted

1½–2 tbsp cornstarch

1 tbsp chopped fresh flat-leaf parsley

pepper

freshly cooked broccoli, to serve

LIMA BEAN PURÉE

10½ oz/300 g canned lima beans, drained and rinsed

2 tbsp water or vegetable stock

2 garlic cloves, crushed

4 spring onions, trimmed and chopped

2–3 tbsp vegetable stock

1 To make the Lima Bean Purée, place the lima beans in a nonstick pan with the water and garlic cloves. Heat for 3–4 minutes, or until piping hot, then drain. Mash, then season with pepper. Stir in 4 trimmed and chopped scallions and the stock.

2 Heat the oil in a large nonstick skillet and seal the chicken over medium heat until browned all over. Remove and set aside.

3 Add the onion and garlic to the skillet and cook over medium heat for 3 minutes, stirring frequently. Return the chicken to the skillet together with the red bell pepper strips, the stock, and the red wine. Season with pepper to taste.

4 Bring to a boil, then reduce the heat to a simmer and cover. Cook for 15 minutes, turning the chicken over halfway through the cooking time. Add the olives and cook for an additional 3–5 minutes, or until the chicken is thoroughly cooked.

5 Blend the cornstarch with 3 tablespoons of water to a smooth paste. Stir into the skillet and cook, stirring, until the liquid thickens. Sprinkle with the parsley and serve with the lima bean purée and broccoli.

Serving Analysis			
Energy (kcals)	193	Protein (grams)	25.3
Total fat (grams)	2.8	Carbohydrate (grams)	11.7
of which saturated fat (grams)	0.5	of which sugars (grams)	3.5
Fat/100 g product (grams)	**1.3**		

Grilled Scallops with Bacon

Scallops are far more readily available now than in the past, as most of those on sale are farmed. Look out for king scallops, which are larger than the queen scallops. Choose ones that still retain their coral, the orange piece that is attached.

Cook's Tip

If liked, add some strips of peeled yellow bell pepper and some halved cherry tomatoes to the salad and replace the bread with baby new potatoes.

SERVES 4

8–12 large scallops with corals

2 tbsp orange juice

1 tbsp light soy sauce

8–12 lean Canadian bacon slices, fat discarded

3¹/₂ oz/100 g mixed salad greens, including small beet leaves and mizuna

pepper

TO SERVE

balsamic vinegar

warm whole-wheat bread (optional)

1 Lightly rinse the scallops and remove the dark vein if necessary. Place in a shallow dish. Blend the orange juice and soy sauce and pour over the scallops. Season with pepper. Cover and let stand in the refrigerator for 30 minutes. Drain.

2 Lightly stretch the bacon slices with the back of a knife. Cut in half. Wrap two halves round each scallop. Thread onto small wooden skewers, leaving a little space between each (this will ensure that the scallops cook evenly).

3 Heat a stovetop grill pan or griddle until smoking, then cook the wrapped scallops for 6–8 minutes, or until cooked. Turn the scallops frequently as they cook.

4 Arrange the salad greens on serving platters. Remove the scallops from the skewers and place on top of the salad greens. Drizzle with a little balsamic vinegar and serve with warm whole-wheat bread.

Serving Analysis			
Energy (kcals)	113	Protein (grams)	18.3
Total fat (grams)	3.1	Carbohydrate (grams)	3.1
of which saturated fat (grams)	1.1	of which sugars (grams)	1.4
Fat/100 g product (grams)	**2.7**		

Warm Beef Niçoise

Ideal to serve when entertaining friends or family at a summer lunch party or an impromptu dinner party.

SERVES 4

4 tenderloin steaks, about 4 oz/115 g each, fat discarded

2 tbsp red wine vinegar

2 tbsp orange juice

2 tsp ready-made English mustard

2 eggs

6 oz/175 g baby new potatoes

4 oz/115 g green beans, trimmed

6 oz/175 g mixed salad greens, such as baby spinach, arugula, and mizuna

1 yellow bell pepper, seeded, peeled, and cut into strips

6 oz/175 g cherry tomatoes, halved

black olives, pitted, to garnish (optional)

2 tsp extra virgin olive oil

pepper

1 Place the steaks in a shallow dish. Blend the vinegar with 1 tablespoon of orange juice and 1 teaspoon of mustard. Pour over the steaks, cover, then let stand in the refrigerator for at least 30 minutes. Turn over halfway through the marinating time.

2 Place the eggs in a pan and cover with cold water. Bring to a boil, then reduce the heat to a simmer and cook for 10 minutes. Remove and plunge the eggs into cold water. Once cold, shell and set aside.

3 Meanwhile, place the potatoes in a pan and cover with cold water. Bring to a boil, then cover and let simmer for 15 minutes, or until tender when pierced with a fork. Drain and set aside.

4 Bring a pan of water to a boil. Add the beans, then cover and let simmer for 5–8 minutes, or until tender. Drain, then plunge into cold water. Drain again and set aside. Meanwhile, arrange all the vegetables on top of the salad greens together with the pepper, cherry tomatoes, and olives, if using. Blend the remaining orange juice and mustard with the olive oil and set aside.

5 Heat a stovetop grill pan or griddle until smoking. Drain the steaks and cook for 3–5 minutes on each side or according to personal preference. Slice the steaks and arrange on top of the salad, then pour over the dressing and serve.

Serving Analysis

Energy (kcals)	281	Protein (grams)	30.8
Total fat (grams)	11.3	Carbohydrate (grams)	13.5
of which saturated fat (grams)	4.3	of which sugars (grams)	6.6
Fat/100 g product (grams)	3		

Sole and Orange with Wilted Swiss Chard

10 minutes

50 minutes

GI   low

This makes a good lunch dish, as it is both quick and easy to prepare and cook, leaving you plenty of time to chat to your guests.

SERVES 4

8 sole fillets

1½ tbsp finely grated orange rind

10 oz/280 g Swiss chard, thoroughly rinsed

6 scallions, trimmed and finely chopped

2 tbsp orange juice

1 tbsp lemon juice (optional)

1 lb/450 g baby new potatoes

10 oz/280 g baby carrots, scrubbed

6 oz/175 g shelled shrimp, thawed if frozen

pepper

Cook's Tip

Take care not to overcook the packages once you have added the shrimp, or the shrimp will be tough and tasteless. They just need reheating.

1 Preheat the oven to 350°F/180°C. Rinse the sole fillets and pat dry with paper towels. Mix half the orange rind with some pepper and sprinkle over each fillet. Set aside. Remove the white ribs from the Swiss chard and shred the green leaves. Cut out 4 squares of parchment paper or foil, 8-inch/20-cm in diameter, and divide the leaves between the sheets. Place 2 sole fillets on top of each and sprinkle over two-thirds of the scallions and a little orange juice, then fold the paper over to form a package. Place in a baking pan. Cook in the oven for 10 minutes. Cut the ribs of the chard into small pieces and rinse, then cook in boiling water with the lemon juice for 15–20 minutes, or until tender. Drain and keep warm.

2 Meanwhile, cook the potatoes in boiling water over medium heat for 15 minutes, or until tender when pierced with a fork. Drain and lightly crush with a potato masher. Stir in the remaining scallions and season with pepper. Keep warm. At the same time, cook the carrots in boiling water for 10–15 minutes, or until tender when pierced with a fork. Drain and sprinkle with the remaining rind. Keep warm.

3 Remove the fish packages from the oven and carefully open them. Scatter the shelled shrimp over the fish. Fold the packages again and return to the oven for an additional 5 minutes. Remove and place a package on each plate. Serve with the cooked white Swiss chard ribs, and the potatoes and carrots.

Serving Analysis

Energy (kcals)	256	Protein (grams)	32.3
Total fat (grams)	3.2	Carbohydrate (grams)	25.9
of which saturated fat (grams)	0.5	of which sugars (grams)	8.8
Fat/100 g product (grams)	**0.7**		

15 minutes

25 minutes

GI low

Cod with Herb Crust

This is a perfect supper dish for the whole family. Other white fish can be used for this recipe, if preferred. If you use sole, flounder, or halibut, cook slightly less.

.Cook's Tip

Take care not to overcook the fish, or it will be dry. Pierce the salmon with a sharp knife: if it goes in easily with no resistance, the fish is cooked.

SERVES 4

4 pieces cod loin, about 4 oz/115 g each

4 garlic cloves

1 tbsp finely grated orange rind

2 tbsp chopped fresh parsley

2 tbsp chopped fresh dill

2 tbsp chopped fresh tarragon

4 tbsp orange juice

4 large tomatoes

pepper

TO SERVE

lima bean purée

freshly cooked green beans

1 Preheat the oven to 400°F/200°C. Lightly rinse the fish and pat dry with paper towels. Crush 2 of the garlic cloves and mix with the orange rind, the herbs, and a little pepper, then press one-quarter of the herb mixture onto each piece of fish. Place the fish in an ovenproof dish and pour the orange juice round them.

2 Rinse and dry the tomatoes and cut in half. Cut the remaining garlic cloves into thin slivers and insert 3–4 slivers into each tomato half. Place in an ovenproof dish.

3 Place the fish in the oven and cook for 10 minutes, then add the tomatoes and cook with the fish for an additional 10 minutes, or until the fish is cooked.

4 Serve with lima bean purée, the roasted tomatoes, and green beans.

Serving Analysis			
Energy (kcals)	107	Protein (grams)	21.9
Total fat (grams)	0.9	Carbohydrate (grams)	3
of which saturated fat (grams)	0.1	of which sugars (grams)	1.5
Fat/100 g product (grams)	**0.6**		

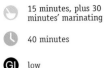

15 minutes, plus 30 minutes' marinating

40 minutes

GI low

Turkey with Roasted Vegetables

Turkey is a good choice when trying to keep down the fat content of your diet, as it is one of the leanest meats. Don't serve it only for Thanksgiving—try using some of the many various cuts that are now readily available.

SERVES 4

4 skinless turkey breast fillets, about 4 oz/115 g each

1 fresh red chili, seeded

4 garlic cloves, peeled

1 onion, cut into wedges

1 zucchini, cut into chunks

1 red bell pepper, seeded and cut into thick strips

1 yellow bell pepper, seeded and cut into thick wedges

1–2 tbsp extra virgin olive oil

8 oz/225 g vine-ripened cherry or small plum tomatoes

1 tbsp shredded fresh basil

pepper

10 oz/280 g freshly cooked tagliatelle, to serve

1 Preheat the oven to 375°F/190°C. Lightly rinse the turkey breast fillets and pat dry with paper towels. Finely chop the chili and crush 2 of the garlic cloves, then mix together and rub over the turkey. Place on a plate and cover loosely with parchment paper, then let stand in the refrigerator for 30 minutes.

2 Cut the remaining garlic cloves in half and place in a roasting pan with the remaining prepared vegetables except for the tomatoes, then drizzle over one tablespoon of the oil. Grind over some pepper.

3 Roast in the preheated oven for 15 minutes, turning the vegetables over occasionally. Place the turkey steaks on top and continue to roast for 15 minutes, then add the tomatoes and roast for an additional 10 minutes, or until the turkey is thoroughly cooked. Sprinkle with the shredded basil and serve with freshly cooked tagliatelle.

Serving Analysis			
Energy (kcals)	201	Protein (grams)	31.1
Total fat (grams)	4.3	Carbohydrate (grams)	10
of which saturated fat (grams)	0.9	of which sugars (grams)	8
Fat/100 g product (grams)	**1.3**		

Aromatic Chicken Packages

15 minutes

50 minutes

GI low

The aromatic flavors of the East can be used to great effect in both savory and sweet dishes. Here the chicken is delicately spiced and enhanced by the use of spices also in the rice.

SERVES 4

4 skinless, boneless chicken breasts, about 4 oz/115 g each

1 tsp or fine spray extra virgin olive oil

1 zucchini, trimmed

1 carrot

1 celery stalk, trimmed

1 small red bell pepper, seeded

2 cinnamon sticks, broken in half

10 cardamom pods, lightly cracked

4 tbsp white wine

1 tbsp chopped cilantro

scant 1 cup brown basmati rice

few saffron strands

pepper

Cook's Tip

Fish such as salmon steaks, swordfish steaks, or flounder fillets can be used in place of the chicken. The cooking times may need to be adjusted.

1 Preheat the oven to 375°F/190°C. Cut 4 square sheets of parchment paper, 8 inches/20 cm in size. Lightly rinse the chicken and pat dry with paper towels. Heat a nonstick skillet, add the oil, then brown the chicken on all sides. Set aside.

2 Cut all the vegetables into thin strips. In the center of each square of baking parchment, place one quarter of the vegetable strips with a chicken breast on top. Place half a cinnamon stick and 2 cardamom pods on each chicken breast. Pour over 1 tablespoon of the wine, then season with a little pepper and add a little chopped cilantro. Fold over to encase the vegetables and chicken. Place the chicken parcels in a large baking pan and cook in the preheated oven for 20 minutes, or until thoroughly cooked. Remove the packages from the oven and place each one on a serving plate, letting each person appreciate the aroma as they open their own package.

3 Meanwhile, rinse the rice, then place in a pan with the remaining cardamom pods and the saffron strands. Cover with water and bring to a boil. Cover, then reduce the heat to a simmer, and cook for 20–25 minutes, or until tender. Drain and place in a warmed serving bowl, then serve with the chicken.

Serving Analysis

Energy (kcals)	335	Protein (grams)	32
Total fat (grams)	2.6	Carbohydrate (grams)	40.5
of which saturated fat (grams)	0.5	of which sugars (grams)	5.3
Fat/100 g product (grams)	**0.9**		

15 minutes, plus 30 minutes' marinating

1 hour

GI low

Grilled Duck with Apricot Relish

Whether you use a stovetop grill pan or a griddle, ensure that it is piping hot so that the food does not stick—there is no need to use any oil or fat.

SERVES 4

4 boneless duck breasts

1¼ cups orange juice

2 garlic cloves, crushed

2 tbsp balsamic vinegar

scant 1 cup Puy lentils

1 tbsp orange zest

orange wedges, to garnish

cherry tomato salad, to serve

APRICOT RELISH

1 onion, thinly sliced

⅓ cup dried apricots, finely chopped

1 tsp brown sugar

1 Remove the skin and fat from the duck breasts and rinse lightly. Pat dry with paper towels, then make 3 diagonal slashes across each. Place in a dish, then blend together 2 tablespoons of the orange juice, the garlic, and 1 tablespoon of the vinegar and pour over. Cover loosely and leave in the refrigerator for 30 minutes.

2 To make the relish, sauté the onion in a nonstick pan over gentle heat for 5 minutes, stirring occasionally. Add the apricots and ½ cup of orange juice, then let simmer for 10 minutes. Stir in the sugar and the remaining vinegar and simmer for 5 minutes, or until the mixture has reduced and thickened. Add a little more orange juice if the consistency becomes too dry and reduce the heat a little.

3 Rinse the lentils, then place in a pan with the remaining orange juice and zest and enough water to cover. Bring to a boil, then cover and let simmer for 30 minutes, or until tender. Meanwhile, heat a stovetop grill pan or griddle until smoking, then drain the duck thoroughly and cook in the pan for 4–5 minutes on each side, or until cooked to personal preference. Cut the duck into thin slices and drain the cooked lentils, then transfer to warmed serving plates. Garnish with orange wedges and serve with relish and the cherry tomato salad.

Serving Analysis			
Energy (kcals)	349	Protein (grams)	34.7
Total fat (grams)	8.3	Carbohydrate (grams)	40.5
of which saturated fat (grams)	1.6	of which sugars (grams)	15.8
Fat/100 g product (grams)	3		

vegetables and vegetarian

Eggplant Medley

15 minutes

25 minutes

GI low

Eggplants are a very versatile vegetable and can be served in a variety of ways. They can also be made into delicious dips, and the roasted flesh is an ideal thickening agent for casseroles.

SERVES 4

1 large eggplant, weighing about 10 oz/280 g, sliced

1 tbsp extra virgin olive oil

1 onion, cut into wedges

2–4 garlic cloves, cut in half

1 red bell pepper, seeded, peeled, and chopped

1 yellow bell pepper, seeded, peeled, and chopped

scant 1 cup vegetable stock

4 oz/115 g white mushrooms

5 cups baby spinach leaves, rinsed

3 oz/85 g goat cheese, sliced

whole-wheat bread, to serve

Cook's Tip

If baby spinach is unavailable, use leaf spinach and shred before using.

1 Heat the oil in a large skillet and add the eggplant with the onion and garlic. Cook over very gentle heat for 10 minutes, stirring frequently, then add the bell peppers. Pour in the stock and bring to a boil, then reduce the heat, cover, and let simmer for 10 minutes.

2 Add the mushrooms and continue to simmer for 5 minutes, then stir in the spinach and cook, uncovered, stirring occasionally until the spinach has begun to wilt.

3 Place the goat cheese slices on top, then heat for 1–2 minutes, or until the cheese begins to melt. Serve immediately with chunks of whole-wheat bread.

Serving Analysis			
Energy (kcals)	132	Protein (grams)	7.2
Total fat (grams)	7.5	Carbohydrate (grams)	9.6
of which saturated fat (grams)	2.8	of which sugars (grams)	7.9
Fat/100 g product (grams)	**2.7**		

15 minutes

2 hours

GI low

Stuffed Large Zucchini

Although large zucchini seem to have gone out of fashion, they are available virtually throughout the year, from supermarkets, farm stores, or farmers' markets, and they are also really easy to grow yourself.

SERVES 4

generous ³/₈ cup green lentils

1 tsp extra virgin olive oil

1 onion, finely chopped

2–3 garlic cloves, crushed

1 celery stalk, chopped

1 carrot, grated

1 tbsp chopped fresh rosemary

1 egg white, beaten

scant 1 cup vegetable stock

1 large zucchini, weighing 2 lb/900 g

2 beefsteak tomatoes, thickly sliced

1 oz/25 g sharp half-fat Cheddar cheese, grated

pepper

freshly cooked carrots, to serve

1 Preheat the oven to 350°F/180°C. Rinse the lentils and place in a pan. Cover with water and bring to a boil, then cook for 10 minutes. Reduce the heat, then cover and let simmer for 35 minutes, or until soft. Drain thoroughly and set aside.

2 Heat the oil in a pan and sauté the onion, garlic, celery, and carrot for 5 minutes, or until softened. Stir in the lentils with the rosemary, and season with pepper to taste. Remove from the heat and add the egg white and enough stock to moisten the mixture.

3 Peel the large zucchini if preferred and cut into 2-inch/5-cm thick rings. Remove the seeds, then place in an ovenproof dish large enough to hold all the rings. Stuff the hollows with the lentil mixture. Place a tomato slice on each ring and pour round the remaining stock, then cover with foil.

4 Cook in the preheated oven for 1 hour, or until the marrow feels tender when pierced with the tip of a sharp knife. Remove the foil and sprinkle the tomato with the grated cheese. Return to the oven for an additional 5 minutes. Serve with the freshly cooked carrots.

Serving Analysis			
Energy (kcals)	153	Protein (grams)	10.6
Total fat (grams)	3.2	Carbohydrate (grams)	22
of which saturated fat (grams)	0.8	of which sugars (grams)	9.9
Fat/100 g product (grams)	**0.8**		

20 minutes, plus cooling time

1 hour 10 minutes

GI low

Lentil and Asparagus Quiche

Red split lentils are best for this quiche base and can be easily molded into the tart pan.

SERVES 6

Cook's Tip

If possible use a smooth-sided pan, as this will make the quiche easier to remove.

1¹⁄₈ cups red split lentils

1 tbsp chopped fresh basil

3 egg whites plus 2 whole eggs

4 oz/115 g baby asparagus spears

1 red bell pepper, seeded, peeled, and cut into strips

1 orange bell pepper, seeded, peeled, and cut into strips

4 scallions, trimmed and diagonally sliced

8 black olives, pitted

1¹⁄₂ oz/40 g feta cheese (drained weight), crumbled

8 tbsp lowfat cream cheese

pepper

TO SERVE

salad

whole-wheat bread

1 Preheat the oven to 375°F/190°C. Rinse the lentils and place in a pan, then cover with cold water. Bring to a boil and cover, then reduce the heat to a simmer and cook for 12–14 minutes, or until soft. Drain off any excess water and let cool. When cool, stir in the pepper to taste, the basil, and 2 of the egg whites. Mix well, then press into a 8-inch/20-cm loose-bottom tart pan. Bake in the oven for 25–30 minutes, or until the base feels dry. Remove and set aside.

2 Trim the asparagus spears to fit the quiche, then cook in lightly boiling water for 4 minutes. Drain, then plunge into cold water. Drain again and arrange in the base of the quiche. Cover with the bell pepper strips, the scallions, olives, and feta.

3 Beat the 2 whole eggs with the remaining egg white and pepper to taste, then stir in the cream cheese. Spoon over the asparagus mixture, then bake in the preheated oven for 25–30 minutes, or until set. Serve with salad and warm chunks of whole-wheat bread.

Serving Analysis			
Energy (kcals)	198	Protein (grams)	18.2
Total fat (grams)	2.3	Carbohydrate (grams)	28
of which saturated fat (grams)	1.1	of which sugars (grams)	7.4
Fat/100 g product (grams)	**1.1**		

Asian Stir-Fried Vegetables

15 minutes

8 minutes

GI low

This recipe can be used as an accompaniment or as a main meal. If using as a main meal, add either some diced tofu for vegetarians or strips of lean meat or fish for others.

SERVES 4

2 tsp sunflower-seed or corn oil

2 lemon grass stalks, outer leaves removed and chopped

2–4 garlic cloves, crushed

1 Thai chili, seeded and chopped

1 tbsp grated fresh gingerroot

1 red bell pepper, seeded and cut into strips

1 yellow bell pepper, seeded and cut into strips

1 orange bell pepper, seeded and cut into strips

4 oz/115 g zucchini, cut into strips

6 scallions, diagonally sliced

4 oz/115 g bok choy, thoroughly washed, drained, and shredded

generous ½ cup bean sprouts

1 tbsp light soy sauce

1 tbsp medium sherry

freshly cooked brown basmati rice or Japanese soba noodles, to serve

Cook's Tip

It is important to preheat the wok before adding the oil. This ensures that the food does not stick. When stir-frying, use a large spatula and stir constantly, tossing the food around in the wok.

1 Preheat a wok and, when hot, add the sunflower-seed oil and heat for an additional 15 seconds. Add the lemon grass, garlic, chili, and ginger and stir-fry over high heat for 1 minute. Add the bell pepper and zucchini strips and stir-fry for 2 minutes.

2 Add the scallions and continue to stir-fry for an additional 2 minutes before adding the bok choy and bean sprouts. Stir-fry for 1 minute.

3 Blend the soy sauce with the sherry and add to the wok. Stir-fry for 1 minute, or until the vegetables are just cooked. Serve with freshly cooked basmati rice or Japanese soba noodles.

Serving Analysis			
Energy (kcals)	81	Protein (grams)	3.7
Total fat (grams)	2.3	Carbohydrate (grams)	11.2
of which saturated fat (grams)	0.3	of which sugars (grams)	9.3
Fat/100 g product (grams)	1		

15–20 minutes

🕐 15 minutes

GI low

Warm Bean Salad

This salad is delicious whether served warm or cold. If you wish to serve it warm, prepare all the ingredients ahead of time, then when you are ready to eat, it will be no effort at all to cook the salad and serve it in minutes.

SERVES 6

1 tsp olive oil

1 red onion, peeled and finely chopped

2–3 garlic cloves, peeled and chopped

1 fresh red chili, seeded and chopped

1 red bell pepper, seeded and peeled

1 orange bell pepper, seeded and peeled

10$\frac{1}{2}$ oz/300 g canned red kidney beans, drained and thoroughly rinsed

10$\frac{1}{2}$ oz/300 g can black-eye peas, drained and thoroughly rinsed

10$\frac{1}{2}$ oz/300 g can flageolets, drained and thoroughly rinsed

scant 1 cup strained canned tomatoes or tomato juice

1 tbsp sweet chili sauce

3$\frac{1}{2}$ oz/100 g cherry tomatoes, halved

1 tbsp freshly chopped cilantro

salt and pepper

warm strips of pita bread, to serve

Cook's Tip

If liked, pass half the bean mixture through a food processor to form a chunky purée (you may need extra strained canned tomatoes when blending). Return to the pan with the remaining whole beans and heat through gently.

1 Heat the oil in a large pan and gently sauté the onion, garlic, and chili for 3 minutes, stirring frequently. Cut the red and yellow bell peppers into thin strips and thoroughly drain the beans.

2 Add the bell peppers and beans to the pan together with the strained canned tomatoes and sweet chili sauce, and season to taste. Bring to a boil, then reduce the heat and cook for 10 minutes, or until the beans are piping hot. Add the halved tomatoes and heat gently for 2 minutes. Spoon into a serving bowl and sprinkle with the chopped cilantro. Serve warm with strips of pita bread.

Serving Analysis			
Energy (kcals)	128	Protein (grams)	8.0
Total fat (grams)	1.2	Carbohydrate (grams)	17.4
of which saturated fat (grams)	0.3	of which sugars (grams)	7.1
Fat/100 g product (grams)	**0.7**		

Fennel and Lentil Loaf

This is a versatile vegetarian main course, which meat eaters will also enjoy. It is equally good eaten hot or cold.

SERVES 6

generous 1⅛ cups red split lentils

1 small fennel bulb, trimmed and cut into thin wedges

1 yellow bell pepper, seeded and peeled

1 red bell pepper, seeded and peeled

1 small onion, finely chopped

2 garlic cloves, crushed

1 tbsp chopped fresh cilantro

2 oz/55 g half-fat Cheddar cheese, grated

1 egg

freshly cooked cabbage, to serve

SAUCE

2 red bell peppers, seeded and peeled

1 small onion, finely chopped

1¼ cups vegetable stock

1 tbsp tomato paste

pepper

1 Preheat the oven to 375°F/190°C. Line the bottom of a 2-lb/900-g loaf pan with a piece of nonstick parchment paper. Rinse the lentils and place in a pan, then cover with water and cook for 25–30 minutes, or until soft. Drain thoroughly.

2 Meanwhile, cook the fennel in boiling water for 5 minutes, then drain and place in a bowl. Cut the yellow bell pepper and red bell pepper into strips, then add to the fennel wedges and set aside.

3 Add the onion to the lentil mixture together with the garlic, cilantro, and cheese. Season with pepper to taste. Stir in the egg and mix well. Place half of the mixture in the bottom of the pan, then arrange the fennel wedges and bell pepper strips on top. Spoon the remaining lentil mixture on top and smooth the top. Bake in the oven for 45–50 minutes, or until the top of the loaf feels firm.

4 Make the sauce by simmering the remaining bell peppers and onion in the stock for 10 minutes, or until very soft. Stir in the tomato paste and let simmer for an additional 5 minutes. Pass through a food processor and then, if a smooth sauce is preferred, rub through a fine strainer. Season with pepper to taste, then serve with the cooked loaf and freshly cooked cabbage.

Serving Analysis			
Energy (kcals)	207	Protein (grams)	15
Total fat (grams)	3.6	Carbohydrate (grams)	30.5
of which saturated fat (grams)	1.3	of which sugars (grams)	8.9
Fat/100 g product (grams)	**1.8**		

Red Cabbage Slaw

20 minutes

no cooking required

GI low

Ideal for any occasion, as part of a buffet, or even eaten on its own as a lunchtime snack, this can also be turned into a main meal salad by simply adding a little cheese or a few nuts.

SERVES 6

1 lb/450 g red cabbage

1 eating apple

4 tbsp orange juice

1 large carrot, peeled and grated

1 red onion, peeled and cut into tiny wedges

6 oz/175 g cherry tomatoes, halved

3-inch/7.5-cm piece cucumber, peeled if preferred and diced

1/3 cup fresh dates, pitted and chopped

1 tbsp extra virgin olive oil

1 tbsp chopped fresh flat-leaf parsley

pepper

Cook's Tip

Vary the ingredients used—try a mix of both red and hard white cabbage. Add some peeled chopped bell peppers, or radishes, grated celery root, or shredded bok choy.

1 Discard the outer leaves and hard central core from the cabbage and shred finely. Wash thoroughly in plenty of cold water, then shake dry and place in a salad bowl.

2 Core the apple and chop, toss in 1 tablespoon of the orange juice, then add to the salad bowl together with the carrot, onion, tomatoes, cucumbers, and dates.

3 Place the remaining orange juice in a screw-top jar, add the oil, parsley, and pepper and shake until blended. Pour the dressing over the salad and toss lightly, then serve.

Serving Analysis			
Energy (kcals)	78	Protein (grams)	1.8
Total fat (grams)	2.4	Carbohydrate (grams)	13.3
of which saturated fat (grams)	0.3	of which sugars (grams)	12.6
Fat/100 g product (grams)	**1.1**		

15 minutes

5 minutes

GI low

Asparagus, Spinach, and Cherry Tomato Salad

Asparagus is now readily available throughout the year and, although it is expensive, only a small quantity is required for this recipe and it is well worth the expense. Look for homegrown asparagus during May and early June.

Cook's Tip

If liked, use fine green beans in place of the asparagus. Prepare as for the asparagus, discarding the stalk end of the bean.

SERVES 4

6 oz/175 g baby or fine asparagus spears

5 cups baby spinach leaves

2 heads chicory

8 scallions, trimmed and chopped

1 small bunch radishes, trimmed and halved

8 oz/225 g cherry tomatoes, halved

14 oz/400 g canned red kidney beans, drained and rinsed

DRESSING

1 tbsp extra virgin olive oil

3 tbsp orange juice

1 tsp whole-grain mustard

1 tbsp balsamic vinegar

1 Trim the asparagus spears if necessary, then cook in gently simmering water for 3–5 minutes, or until just tender. Drain, then plunge into cold water. Drain again and set aside. Lightly rinse the spinach leaves and shake dry. Arrange in a salad bowl or on a large platter.

2 Divide the chicory into leaves, rinse, and shake dry. Arrange with the drained asparagus on top of the spinach.

3 Place the scallions, the radishes, cherry tomatoes, and red kidney beans in a bowl and toss lightly. Arrange on the salad with the asparagus and chicory. Place all the dressing ingredients together in a screw-top jar and shake vigorously. Pour over the salad and serve.

Serving Analysis			
Energy (kcals)	175	Protein (grams)	11
Total fat (grams)	4.6	Carbohydrate (grams)	23.7
of which saturated fat (grams)	0.7	of which sugars (grams)	9.1
Fat/100 g product (grams)	**1.4**		

Beet with Orange

The combination of beet and orange may seem a little strange, but it is absolutely delicious. Make sure to use fresh beet rather than beet that has been pickled in vinegar.

SERVES 4

1 lb/450 g cooked fresh beet

1 small orange

1 oz/25 g half-fat Cheddar cheese

few mixed salad greens

1–2 tsp extra virgin olive oil

1 tbsp snipped fresh chives

pepper

1 Peel the beet, discarding the root and skin, then cut into small dice or slices. Peel the orange over a bowl to catch the juice, then divide into segments, taking care to discard the bitter white pith and as much of the membrane as possible. Cut the segments in half. Cut the cheese into small pieces.

2 Place the salad greens in a serving bowl. Arrange the beet and orange segments on top, then scatter over the cheese.

3 Drizzle over the oil and sprinkle with the chives and the reserved orange juice, then season to taste with pepper. Serve immediately.

Cook's Tip

Raw beet can be cooked in the oven, on the stove, or in the microwave. Cut off the leaves about 1 inch/2.5 cm from the top of the beet. Scrub well, taking care not to damage the skin. To cook in the oven, wrap the beet in foil, and cook in a preheated oven at 375°F/190°C for 1 hour, or until cooked. To cook on the stove, put the beet in a pan and cover with cold water, then bring to a boil. Cover, reduce the heat to a simmer and cook for 1 hour, or until tender. To microwave, place the beet in a bowl and cover with microwave film that is lightly pierced, and then cook on High for 14–20 minutes, or until cooked. Let stand until cool enough to handle.

Serving Analysis			
Energy (kcals)	76	Protein (grams)	4.3
Total fat (grams)	1.9	Carbohydrate (grams)	11.2
of which saturated fat (grams)	0.7	of which sugars (grams)	10.6
Fat/100 g product (grams)	**1.2**		

6

desserts and bakes

Sparkling Melon Cups

15 minutes

10 minutes, plus
2 hours' setting

GI medium

This is a perfect dessert to serve on a hot summer's day, either for an informal lunch or a more formal dinner party.

SERVES 4

2 cups Champagne or sparkling white wine

1–2 tsp honey, or to taste

1 sachet (¼ oz/5 g) gelatin

3 tbsp brandy or Cointreau, or use extra wine

2 wedges assorted melons, such as Galia, Ogen, or Cantaloupe

¾ cup fresh raspberries

1 Pour the Champagne into a heavy-bottom pan and add the honey, then sprinkle in the gelatin. Place over gentle heat and bring to a boil, whisking throughout. Remove and continue to whisk for 2 minutes, or until the gelatin has completely dissolved. Stir in the brandy, then pour into a pitcher and let stand until cold.

2 Discard the skin and any seeds from the melon wedges and cut into small dice. Arrange with the raspberries in wide-rimmed cocktail or similar glasses, or in individual glass dishes.

3 Once the jelly is cold, pour over the fruit and let stand in the refrigerator for 2 hours, or until set.

Cook's Tip

For a change, cut the melon into thin wedges and arrange in alternating colors in a mold or 2-lb/900-g loaf pan. Pour over the cold jelly and cover with plastic wrap and clean weights and let set. Other fruits can be added or used. Do not use citrus and kiwifruits, however—these will stop the jelly from setting.

Serving Analysis			
Energy (kcals)	128	Protein (grams)	2.2
Total fat (grams)	0.1	Carbohydrate (grams)	11.6
of which saturated fat (grams)	0	of which sugars (grams)	11.6
Fat/100 g product (grams)	**0.1**		

Carrot Cake

Carrot cake is a perennial, universal favorite that is ideal for any occasion. When you are looking for a treat, look no farther than this recipe.

Cook's Tip

If liked as a dessert, serve the cake squares warm with a spoonful of lowfat plain or strained plain yogurt, or lowfat cream cheese.

MAKES 12 SQUARES

2 cups self-rising whole-wheat flour

2¹⁄₂ tsp baking powder

1 tsp ground cinnamon

¹⁄₂ tsp pumpkin pie spice

¹⁄₂ cup wheat bran

generous ³⁄₈ cup packed brown sugar

4 oz/115 g carrots, grated

12 oz/350 g eating apples, peeled, cored, and grated

¹⁄₂ cup raisins

scant 1 cup dried apricots, finely chopped

1 egg, beaten

1 egg white

4 tsp sunflower-seed or corn oil

¹⁄₂ cup orange juice

1 tbsp slivered almonds (optional)

1 Preheat the oven to 350°F/180°C. Lightly oil and line the bottom of a 9 x 13-inch/23 x 33-cm oblong baking pan with nonstick parchment paper. Sift the flour, baking powder, and spices into a mixing bowl, adding any bran residue left in the strainer. Stir in the wheat bran and the sugar. Add the carrots, grated apple, raisins, and apricots and stir well.

2 Beat the egg and egg white together and add to the mixture together with enough oil to give a soft dropping consistency. Spoon into the prepared pan and smooth the top.

3 Sprinkle over the slivered almonds, if using, and bake in the oven for 30–35 minutes, or until risen and the top springs back when touched lightly with a clean finger. Remove from the oven and let cool before cutting into squares and serving.

Serving Analysis			
Energy (kcals)	147	Protein (grams)	4
Total fat (grams)	2.3	Carbohydrate (grams)	29.6
of which saturated fat (grams)	0.3	of which sugars (grams)	17.4
Fat/100 g product (grams)	2.7		

10 minutes

15–20 minutes

GI low

Granola Bars

These bars are ideal for lunch boxes and will give a lift to flagging energy.

MAKES 12 BARS

generous $^3/_8$ cup packed brown sugar

2 tsp baking powder

1 tsp ground cinnamon

$^1/_2$ tsp ground ginger

$2^2/_3$ cups rolled oats

$^1/_2$ cup raisins

generous $^3/_8$ cup pecans, chopped

$^1/_2$ cup dried cranberries

1 egg

1 egg white

$^2/_3$ cup clear unsweetened apple juice

1 Preheat the oven to 400°F/200°C. Line a shallow 8 x 12-inch/20 x 30-cm baking pan with nonstick parchment paper. Mix the sugar, baking powder, and spices in a large bowl. Stir in the oats, raisins, pecans, and cranberries. Beat the egg and egg white together, then add enough apple juice to the mixture to bring the mixture together. Mix well.

2 Press into the prepared pan, smoothing the top with a palette knife, and bake in the preheated oven for 15–20 minutes, or until lightly browned. Remove from the oven and let stand until cold before cutting into bars.

Serving Analysis			
Energy (kcals)	76	Protein (grams)	1.9
Total fat (grams)	1.1	Carbohydrate (grams)	15.8
of which saturated fat (grams)	0.2	of which sugars (grams)	11.6
Fat/100 g product (grams)	**3**		

Berry Sorbet

15 minutes, plus
2–3 hours' freezing

5 minutes

GI medium

This is especially good on long hot summer days when you need something to help you cool down.

SERVES 4

1 lb/450 g mixed summer berries, such as raspberries, strawberries, and blueberries

½ cup red wine

½ cup clear unsweetened apple juice

1–2 tsp honey, or to taste

2 tbsp Kirsch or Cointreau, or use extra apple juice

TO DECORATE

few fresh mint sprigs

extra berries

Cook's Tip

Chill the glasses for 10 minutes before using. Remember to return the freezer to its normal setting.

1 Either turn your freezer to rapid freeze 2 hours before you want to freeze or place the bowl of an ice-cream maker in the freezer overnight. Pick over the berries, hulling any as necessary and cutting any large fruits in half. Rinse lightly.

2 Place the fruits in a heavy-bottom pan and add the wine, apple juice, and honey. Bring to a boil over medium heat and let simmer for 5 minutes. Remove and cool before passing through a food processor and then rubbing through a fine strainer to give a seedless liquid.

3 If you are making the granita without an ice-cream maker, pour the fruit mixture into a freezer container, and place in the freezer for 2–3 hours, or until a frozen slush is formed. Stir every 30 minutes to break up the ice crystals. Alternatively, assemble the ice-cream maker and switch on, then pour in the fruit liquid. Let freeze for 35–45 minutes, or follow the manufacturer's directions, until a frozen slush is formed.

4 Spoon into chilled glasses or individual glass dishes and decorate with mint sprigs or extra berries.

Serving Analysis			
Energy (kcals)	85	Protein (grams)	1.3
Total fat (grams)	0.3	Carbohydrate (grams)	10.6
of which saturated fat (grams)	0.1	of which sugars (grams)	10.6
Fat/100 g product (grams)	**0.1**		

15 minutes, plus
2 hours' cooling

25–35 minutes

GI low

Aromatic Pears

The aromatic spices of the East add an exotic dimension to these pears,
making them absolutely delicious. Try them either warm or chilled with a
spoonful of lowfat plain yogurt.

SERVES 6

6 whole pears, ripe but firm with
  stalks intact

1 tbsp lemon juice

2 tbsp honey

4 whole star anise

2 whole cloves

1 cinnamon stick, bruised

4 green cardamon pods, lightly cracked

2 cups clear unsweetened apple juice

lowfat cream cheese or strained plain
  yogurt, to serve

Cook's Tip

If liked, replace the
apple juice with red or
white wine, though this
can raise the GI rating.

1 Peel the pears, leaving the stalks intact, and place in a large bowl. Cover with
cold water and the lemon juice.

2 Place the honey with the spices and the apple juice in a large heavy-bottom pan
and bring to a boil. Reduce the heat and let simmer for 10 minutes.

3 Drain the pears and add to the pan, standing the pears upright. Cover with a lid,
then let simmer for 15–25 minutes, or until tender when pierced with a skewer.
Remove from the heat and let cool in the syrup, turning the pears or spooning the
syrup occasionally over. Serve with lowfat cream cheese or strained plain yogurt.

Serving Analysis			
Energy (kcals)	88	Protein (grams)	0.7
Total fat (grams)	0.2	Carbohydrate (grams)	22.1
of which saturated fat (grams)	0	of which sugars (grams)	22.1
Fat/100 g product (grams)	**0.1**		

15 minutes, plus 15 minutes' standing

10 minutes

GI medium

Warm Tropical Fruits

This makes a refreshing summer dessert, perfect for eating alfresco. Served slightly warm, these fruits are a delicious end to a perfect day.

SERVES 4

1 ripe mango

1 ripe papaya

8 oz/225 g litchis

1 kiwifruit

2 ripe passion fruit

1 tbsp honey

$2/3$ cup water

half-fat sour cream or % fat cream cheese, to serve

1 Peel the mango, then stand on a cutting board and, with a sharp knife, cut down the fruit as near to the seed as possible. Turn the fruit slightly after each cut. When the fruit has been removed, cut the flesh into small wedges or dice.

2 Cut the papaya in half. Scoop out and discard the seeds, then peel and cut into small wedges or dice.

3 Peel the litchis, then make a small slit down each fruit and carefully remove the pit. Peel the kiwi and cut into small wedges. Set aside.

4 Cut the passion fruit in half and scoop out the flesh and seeds. Place in a heavy-bottom pan with the honey and the water. Place over gentle heat, stirring occasionally, until the honey has dissolved. Bring to a boil and boil for 2 minutes. Reduce the heat to a simmer and heat very gently for 5 minutes. Remove from the heat and let stand for 15 minutes, or until you are ready to heat the fruits.

5 Strain the juice if liked, then return to the pan and discard the passion fruit seeds. Add all the prepared fruits. Let simmer for 3–5 minutes, or until the fruits are warm. Serve with the half-fat sour cream or lowfat cream cheese.

Serving Analysis			
Energy (kcals)	91	Protein (grams)	1.7
Total fat (grams)	0.2	Carbohydrate (grams)	21.7
of which saturated fat (grams)	0	of which sugars (grams)	17.5
Fat/100 g product (grams)	**0.1**		

Baked Peaches

10 minutes

10 minutes

GI low

Although quick and easy to prepare and cook, this provides a stunning and elegant dessert that will be enjoyed by all. Fresh peaches or nectarines, when in season, are best, but if unavailable use peach halves, canned in fruit juice.

SERVES 4

4 large fresh ripe peaches

⅛ cup dried apricots

⅛ cup blueberries

1 tbsp slivered almonds, toasted

2 tbsp medium sherry or orange juice

fresh mint sprigs or lemon balm sprigs, to decorate

lowfat cream cheese or frozen yogurt, to serve

1 Preheat the oven to 350°F/180°C. Cut the peaches in half and remove the pits. Place in an ovenproof dish.

2 Finely chop the apricots and place in a bowl with the blueberries and stir. Use to fill the hollows left by the removal of the peach pits. Sprinkle with the almonds.

3 Pour over the sherry, then bake in the oven for 10 minutes, or until heated through. Serve decorated with mint or lemon balm sprigs and lowfat cream cheese or frozen yogurt.

Cook's Tip

If preferred, peel the peaches. To do this, make a small cross at the stalk end of each fruit. Place the peaches in a large bowl and pour boiling water over them. Let stand for 2 minutes then lift one out and, when cool enough to handle, peel. Repeat with the other peaches.

Serving Analysis

Energy (kcals)	68	Protein (grams)	1.9
Total fat (grams)	2.2	Carbohydrate (grams)	9.1
of which saturated fat (grams)	0.2	of which sugars (grams)	9
Fat/100 g product (grams)	**2.4**		

15 minutes, plus
2 hours' cooling

12–15 minutes

GI low

Fruit Parfait

Fruit Fools can be served for both formal or informal occasions and provide an ideal finale to any meal.

Cook's Tip

How much gelatin you will need depends on the ripeness of the fruit used. Really ripe fruit will produce far more juice, so use the full amount of gelatin. Unripe fruit will need less gelatin and more cooking time to soften.

SERVES 4

12 oz/350 g red plums, pitted

4 tbsp orange juice

2–3 tsp honey, or to taste

12 oz/350 g fresh strawberries, sliced if large

2–3 tsp gelatin

6 tbsp lowfat plain yogurt

TO DECORATE

extra fruit

fresh mint sprigs

1 If the plums are very ripe, peel, then slice and place in a pan with 2 tablespoons of the orange juice and honey. Bring to a boil and reduce the heat, then cover and let simmer for 5–10 minutes, or until soft. Add half the strawberries and let simmer for an additional 5 minutes.

2 Remove and let cool, then blend in a food processor with the remaining strawberries to form a purée.

3 Place the remaining orange juice in a heatproof bowl, placed over a pan of gently simmering water. Sprinkle in the gelatin and stir frequently for about 3 minutes, or until the gelatin is dissolved. Cool then stir into the fruit purée. Let stand until cold.

4 Add the yogurt to the cold purée and stir lightly to give a rippled effect. Spoon into glasses and let chill until required. Serve with extra fruit or fresh mint sprigs.

Serving Analysis			
Energy (kcals)	117	Protein (grams)	6.5
Total fat (grams)	0.8	Carbohydrate (grams)	22.5
of which saturated fat (grams)	0.3	of which sugars (grams)	22.5
Fat/100 g product (grams)	0.3		

Raspberry Sponge Cake

Now and again, everyone needs a comfort hit and this is just the thing: light fluffy sponge, topped with ripe, mouthwatering raspberries, and some half-fat cream cheese. For a real treat, add a sprinkling of grated chocolate.

SERVES 8

2 eggs	1 tbsp cooled boiled water
generous ¼ cup superfine sugar	⅔ cup lowfat cream cheese
1 tsp vanilla extract	2¾ cups fresh raspberries
scant ⅔ cup all-purpose flour	1 tbsp grated semisweet chocolate (optional)

1 Preheat the oven to 425°F/220°C. Lightly oil and line a 10 x 8-inch/25 x 20-cm baking pan with nonstick parchment paper. Place the eggs, sugar, and vanilla extract over a pan of gently simmering water and whisk for 5–8 minutes, or until really thick and creamy.

2 Remove from the heat and continue to whisk until cool. Sift the flour into the mixture and stir in lightly, adding the water. Spoon into the prepared pan and tap the pan lightly on the counter to remove the air bubbles.

3 Bake in the preheated oven for 10–12 minutes, or until well risen and the top springs back when touched lightly with a clean finger. Remove and let cool.

4 When you are ready to serve, discard the lining paper, and cut the cake into 8 squares. Top each square with cream cheese and some raspberries. Sprinkle with a little grated chocolate if liked, and serve.

Serving Analysis			
Energy (kcals)	115	Protein (grams)	4.9
Total fat (grams)	2.4	Carbohydrate (grams)	19.5
of which saturated fat (grams)	0.8	of which sugars (grams)	11.4
Fat/100 g product (grams)	2.5		

Index